Can the Earth Survive?

Population Explosion

Ewan McLeish

rosen publishing's
**rosen
central**

New York

Published in 2010 by The Rosen Publishing Group Inc.
29 East 21st Street, New York, NY 10010

First Edition

Commissioning Editor: Jennifer Sanderson
Consultant: Steph Warren (BA, PGCE, GCSE Principal Examiner)
Cover Designer: Jane Hawkins
Designer: Rob Walster
Picture researcher: Kathy Lockley
Illustrator: Ian Thompson
Proofreader: Susie Brooks

Library of Congress Cataloging-in-Publication Data

McLeish, Ewan, 1950-
    Population explosion / Ewan McLeish. — 1st ed.
      p. cm. — (Can the earth survive?)
    Includes index.
    ISBN 978-1-4358-5356-0 (library binding)
    ISBN 978-1-4358-5488-8 (paperback)
    ISBN 978-1-4358-5489-5 (6-pack)
    1. Overpopulation. I. Title.
    HB871.M3263 2010
    363.9'1—dc22

2008052472

Picture Acknowledgements:
The author and publisher would like to thank the following agencies for allowing these pictures to be
reproduced: Peter Adams/Corbis: 4; Mark Edwards/Still Pictures: 42; Juergen Effner/vari images GmbH & Co
KG/Alamy: 15; Gary Gaugler/Still Pictures: 27; i-Stockphoto cover top left, cover top center, cover top right,
32; Robin Hammond/Panos Pictures: 35; Mark Henley/Panos Pictures: 40; Robert van der Hilst/Corbis: 36;
Manuel Lerida/epa/Corbis: 31; Gerd Ludwig/Visum/ Panos Pictures: 16; M. Timothy O'Keefe/Alamy: 18-19;
Christine Osborne/Ecoscene: 24-25; Stephen Pilick/dpa/Corbis: 29; Reuters/Corbis: 10; Michael
Reynolds/epa/Corbis: Cover, 1; Al Satterwhite/Transtock/Corbis: 7; Qilai Shen/Panos Pictures: 20;
sinopictures/Stuart Forster/ Still Pictures: 44; Friedrich Stark/Alamy: 38; Sean Sutton/MAG/Panos Pictures:
23; David Wall/Alamy: 8

Manufactured in China

Contents

Too Many People?

Every time a person is born or dies, the population changes. In recent years, the world population has been rising so fast that it is often described as a population explosion. The number of people in the world has more than doubled in the last 50 years. But has this happened at a cost to the planet?

Space on Earth

The global population currently stands at 6.7 billion, and it is expected to rise to over 9 billion by 2050. Will this become too much? There are still vast stretches of land that are uninhabited by humans—even in densely populated countries, such as India and the United Kingdom, it is possible to travel for many miles through areas that seem deserted. The problem, then, is not that there is a lack of space on Earth. The real issue tied to the population explosion is the way that people manage Earth's resources—and whether there are enough of these to go around.

IT'S A FACT

Hunger and malnutrition kill almost 6 million children around the world every year.

▼ People crowd a street market in New Delhi, India. As human numbers increase, so will the pressure on the planet to provide the resources that people need to survive.

Evidence

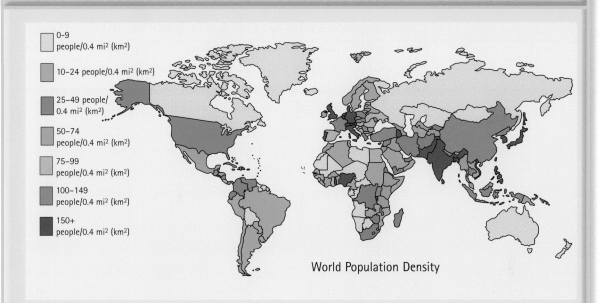

0-9 people/0.4 mi² (km²)

10–24 people/0.4 mi² (km²)

25–49 people/0.4 mi² (km²)

50–74 people/0.4 mi² (km²)

75–99 people/0.4 mi² (km²)

100–149 people/0.4 mi² (km²)

150+ people/0.4 mi² (km²)

World Population Density

DIFFERING DENSITIES

This map of the world shows that the distribution of population density varies dramatically. Southeast Asia and parts of Europe are the most densely populated regions. Other areas, such as the United States and even much of China, have surprisingly low population densities.

Pressure on the Planet

There is now plenty of evidence that human activity is putting a strain on the world's resources. Climate change, partly due to the use of fossil fuels to power cars, homes, and industry, is just one example. Contamination of Earth's water supplies is another major concern, with many people not having access to clean drinking water. The removal of woods and forests to make space for crops or new homes has a huge impact on the environment, and dwindling supplies of the fossil fuels coal, oil, and gas are yet another sign that humans may be asking too much of their planet.

Will problems like these increase as more and more humans inhabit the world, or is there a way to help the Earth deal with them? In order to understand the impact of the population explosion, we need to explore how people organize their societies, interact with the environment, and share what the planet has to offer.

Predicting the Future

There have been many studies on the patterns of population growth—and attempts at predicting the consequences. People who study population trends are called *demographers*. In 1798, the demographer Thomas Malthus published his *Essay on the Principle of Population*. He reasoned that populations tend to grow with the type of upward curve shown in the chart below, and resources—particularly food—tend to follow a linear pattern, more like a straight-line graph. From this, he predicted that the global population would eventually become too large to be supported by the food grown on all available agricultural land. The result would be mass starvation and the dramatic collapse of human numbers.

What Malthus could not predict was the effect of the rapidly developing industrial and agricultural revolutions, which made more resources available than he was able to imagine. In fact, on a global scale, food production has grown faster than the human population. This shows that predicting the future using past or present knowledge is not always reliable.

Evidence

THE WORLD POPULATION

The red line on the graph shows how rapidly the world's population has grown over the last 50 years, and how it is predicted to grow over the next 50 years. The bars show the number of people added to the world's population each year. You will see that these are actually already beginning to decrease.

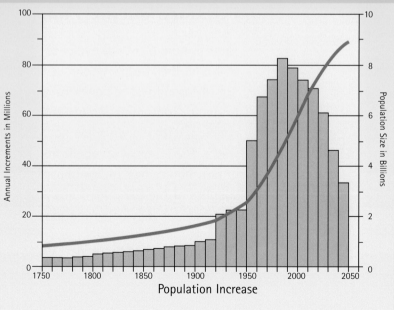

Population Increase

Interdependency

Everything people do is interconnected and has consequences, both for the planet and for other people. Part of the population problem is that Earth's natural resources are not divided equally around the world. For example, few countries are self-sufficient in energy resources, and the use of fossil fuel by the richer, more developed regions of the world continues to damage the Earth as a whole. Similarly, although food supplies globally are not necessarily in short supply, many regions of the world are undernourished because they cannot afford to buy food or it cannot be distributed easily. The issue of overpopulation is therefore a complex one. People may live in an interconnected world, but they also live in an unequal one. This means that the problem of overpopulation needs to be looked at against a background of how the Earth's resources are managed.

▼ The Australian outback is mostly deserted. This is because it is inhospitable and can support very few humans.

What Does Overpopulation Mean?

Overpopulation is the idea that there are too many people living in a given area at a single time. When an area is overpopulated, standards of living fall as resources—and the local environment—are put under too much pressure.

A Question of Quality

Overpopulation is not just about numbers. For example, take a region with a population of 1 million. If the region has sufficient resources for only half a million people, then it is overpopulated—but if there are enough resources for 2 million people, then it is not. This is so regardless of the region's size or population density.

▼ Urban areas such as this one in Melbourne, Australia, are densely populated. The people who live here, however, must be supported by a much larger area to provide basic resources such as food, energy, and water.

Contrasting Countries

Mauritius is a small island off the coast of Africa, with a population density of over 600 people per 0.4 square mile (square kilometer). By most standards, it is a rich land in which the majority of people enjoy a high standard of living, comparable to many countries in the West.

Zimbabwe has a population density of 33 people per 0.4 square mile (square km). Toward the end of the last century, it was exporting so much food it was known as "the breadbasket of southern Africa." But, in 2007, the United Nations (UN) reported that 6 million of its people were threatened by famine and serious food shortages.

Australia is a rich country with a small population for its size—just 2.7 people per 0.4 square mile (square km). Some people believe that Australia cannot sustain its current population without a serious reduction in people's standards of living.

Are any of these countries overpopulated? At first glance, it might seem that Mauritius is facing a population problem, yet its people have a good quality of life. Zimbabwe, on the surface, has enough resources but its people are among the poorest in the world. Australia has a high proportion of land space to people, but its people may now be demanding more than its resources can provide. These examples illustrate how difficult it is to define exactly what overpopulation entails.

The term *resources* goes beyond the basic human necessities of fresh water, clean air, food, shelter, and warmth. It also assumes a reasonable quality of life, including things such as employment, recreation, transportation, education, and medical care. In addition to these, people value open space and pleasant environments, the absence of pollution, such as noise or smoke, and freedom from crime. It is equally important to take into account the needs of the natural world. Local habitats suffer as a result of overpopulation, and this in turn has a negative effect on people's lives.

Overpopulation Effects

One definition of overpopulation suggests that it occurs when the population density is great enough to cause a reduction in quality of life, serious environmental degradation, or long-term shortages of essential goods and services. In some cases, it may have all of these effects, since they are linked. It is also true that any of these effects may also be due to other factors—for example, governments can cause poverty and environmental damage just as effectively as overpopulation.

What Causes Overpopulation?

Whatever its effects, overpopulation can have a variety of causes. It may result from an increase in birth rate, or a decline in mortality (death) rate due to medical advances or improved technology. It may result from an increase in immigration or a decrease in emigration in a particular region. Another cause might be the unsustainable use, and therefore depletion, of resources. None of these causes necessarily depends on human numbers. It is more to do with the relationship between the people and the resources that they have access to.

CASE STUDY
Problems in Ethiopia

Ethiopia's population has grown from 18 million in 1959 to 77 million today. By 2050, there are expected to be 170 million people living in the country. Ethiopia has a history of famine, although it has more fertile land per person than the United Kingdom and a much lower population density.

▲ Famine is still common in Ethiopia, but its causes are complex and not always directly related to high population density.

The causes of famine include state ownership (nationalization) of land, severe droughts, lack of access to fertilizers, military conflicts, and poor government. Is Ethiopia overpopulated? Many people would say, yes. Could Ethiopia support its present population under different circumstances? The answer may be the same.

A Giant Footprint

Resource use within an area is not necessarily limited to what is available locally. High-consuming countries rely on goods and services from all over the world, including less economically developed countries (LEDCs). If consumption by one country depletes resources in another, the second country may suffer the effects of overpopulation. For example, Japan is behind much of the logging that is currently destroying forests in Southeast Asia. This has benefited the economies of some of these Asian countries, but has also led to poverty and displacement of local people, particularly forest dwellers.

A Temporary Phase?

Some people argue that the effects of overpopulation may be temporary. They suggest that when a society is in the early stages of development, the need to gain access to essentials such as food, clean water, and energy, means that damage to the environment is likely to occur. Later in the society's development, with technological and other advances, these so-called "supply" problems are solved and steps are taken to address environmental problems. Examples of this include improvements in air quality, access to safe water, and reduction in pollution in more economically developed countries (MEDCs).

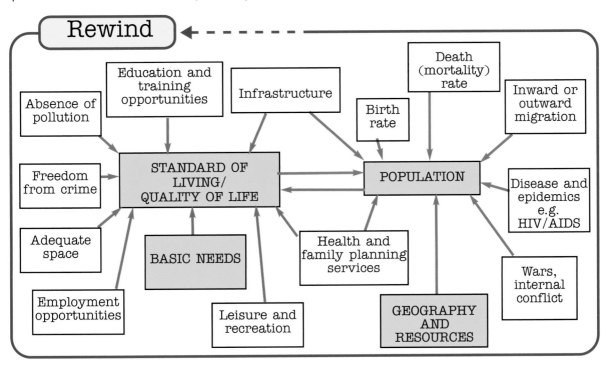

Growing Pains

Population figures vary widely around the world. Before considering the possible solutions to overpopulation, it is important to understand how and where human populations are growing, and why this is.

Population Giants

In 1982, China became the first country to reach a population of 1 billion people. This was despite the fact that some years earlier it had tried to enforce a controversial "one child per family" rule (see page 40). Now China is not alone. In 1999, India also broke through the billion barrier. Both are huge countries, with many resources at their disposal. However, pressure on their resources will increase as populations continue to grow.

Evidence

WHERE IN THE WORLD?

This pie chart of the current world population shows that India and China together make up 35 percent of the global population. Looking at Asia as a whole, this figure rises to almost 60 percent of the global population. Africa and Europe make up 12 percent and 11 percent respectively, with North America (including Canada) contributing around 8 percent. Perhaps surprisingly, the huge continent of South America is home to only 5.3 percent of the world's population.

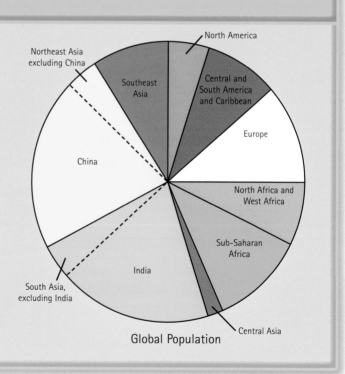

North America
Northeast Asia excluding China
Southeast Asia
Central and South America and Caribbean
Europe
China
North Africa and West Africa
Sub-Saharan Africa
South Asia, excluding India
India
Central Asia

Global Population

Evidence

TOP TEN POPULATIONS

A look at the population figures for individual countries, rather than regions, shows that the United States is the third most populated country in the world. Its population of 300 million is still less than a third of that of India, and less than a quarter of that of China.

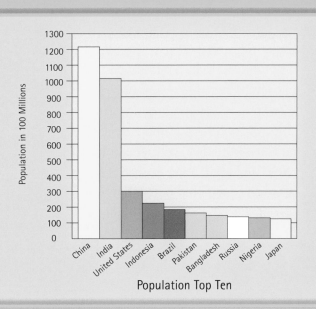

Population Top Ten

Population Density

Population figures are one thing, but what about population densities? Many of the world's largest countries have relatively few people per square mile, despite a high population count overall. The average population density in the United States works out at about 30 people per 0.4 square mile (square km). China has more, at around 138. But this is not especially high compared to smaller countries, such as the United Kingdom and Japan, with 245 and 340 people per 0.4 square mile (square km) respectively. Unlike China, India is very densely populated, at around 350 people per 0.4 sq mile (sq km). Even this seems low in comparison with Bangladesh, however, with an equivalent figure of 1,020.

The differing population densities around the world are partly to do with the natural resources that different countries and regions have available. Habitable land (land that people can live on) is one resource that is lacking, for example, in mountainous and desert regions. Equally significant to population density, however, are social, economic, and political factors. These include access to education and healthcare, trade opportunities, levels of wealth, and the quality of infrastructure, such as transportation and communication systems.

World Population Growth

Although the graphs on pages 12 and 13 show where the largest populations in the world lie, the United Nations (UN) has looked at where in the world the populations are growing fastest.

The UN has predicted that, based on current trends, almost all population growth in the first half of the twenty-first century will take place in LEDCs, such as those in Africa and Asia. They also predict that the population of more developed regions—for example, Europe and North America—will remain largely unchanged. However, between 2005 and 2050, nine countries are expected to contribute half of the world's predicted population increase. These countries are—in order of size of contribution—India, Pakistan, Nigeria, Democratic Republic of Congo, Bangladesh, Uganda, the United States, Ethiopia, and China.

Although the population of many countries is increasing, the UN has also predicted that a number of countries, including Germany, Italy, Japan, and many of the countries making up the former Soviet Union, will have fewer people in 2050 than at the present time.

Evidence

FASTEST GROWERS

The most rapid growth over the past 50 years has been in less developed regions such as Africa (247 percent) and Asia (160 percent). This is compared to 80 percent in North America and 33 percent in Europe. The vertical scale on this graph is called a logarithmic scale, this means the numbers go up more quickly than they appear. The population of Africa is predicted to rise from 200 million in 1950 to ten times that (2 billion) in 2050.

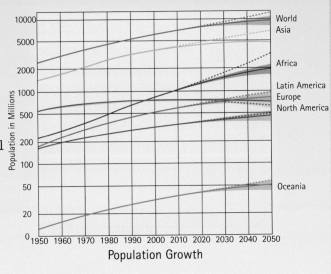

Population Growth

Poor people are often forced to have large families, both as a means of support, and because they lack access to education and information about family planning.

The Reasons Behind the Predictions

Some of the UN predictions on page 14 may seem surprising. For example, with their massive populations, India and China may be expected to make the highest contributions to population increase. However, although this is true for India, China comes only ninth, behind Ethiopia and the United States. Certain parts of the world are not expected to show population increases—some are even likely to decrease in numbers. This is largely due to declining birth rates, as lifestyles—particularly in MEDCs—change. For example, women are expected to have fewer children because they marry later and focus on their careers (see page 36). As for the fastest growers, many will increase quickly, simply because their populations are already vast. The more people there are, the higher the numbers when they multiply. Other factors in LEDCs include lack of education and poor family planning, plus a need for children as a means of labor and "insurance" against poor health.

Already Shrinking

Some countries and regions are already experiencing negative population growth. In parts of Southern Africa, for example, populations are currently declining as a result of high death rates due to HIV/AIDs. This disease has killed millions, especially in poorer countries where adequate treatment is unaffordable or unavailable. Many of the victims are young and may die before they are able to have children. Parts of Eastern Europe, too, are undergoing population decline. In this case, it is due to low fertility rates (the number of births per woman) as the region grapples with economic difficulties.

CASE STUDY
Reducing Russia

Russia's population is shrinking by 700,000 people per year. The giant country's weak national health system and widespread health problems, such as poor nutrition, alcoholism, and exposure to toxic pollutants, mean that infant mortality rates are three times higher than in the West. At the same time, housing shortages, low wages, and poor job security discourage couples from having more children. This may soon change, however, as Russia's improving economy means that people will feel able to have larger families.

Steadying Growth

Average fertility and birth rates are, in fact, falling worldwide. In the 1950s, the average number of children born per woman globally was around five. Today, it is just 2.65, and this is expected to drop to 2.05 by 2050. This is having an effect on overall population growth. The rate of growth has been steadily declining since a peak in 1963. By 2050, it is expected to fall further, to a growth of 34 million people per year in contrast to the current figure of 75 million per year.

In the meantime, life expectancies are rising and death rates are lowering with improved standards of living and healthcare. This increases population figures in the higher age brackets. It will, therefore, take a long time for the population to "break even," despite fewer babies being born each year.

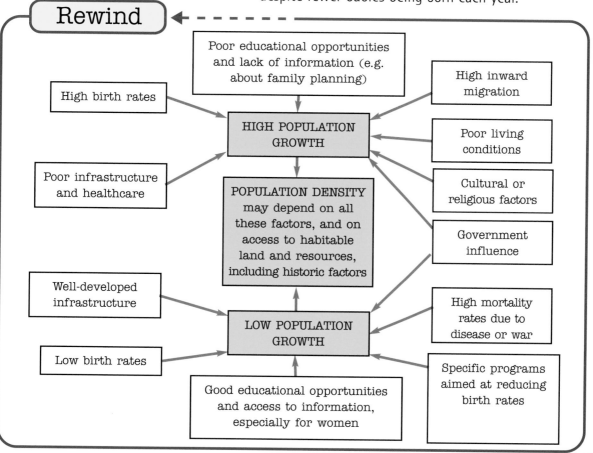

Rewind

Poor educational opportunities and lack of information (e.g. about family planning)

High birth rates

High inward migration

HIGH POPULATION GROWTH

Poor living conditions

Poor infrastructure and healthcare

Cultural or religious factors

POPULATION DENSITY may depend on all these factors, and on access to habitable land and resources, including historic factors

Government influence

Well-developed infrastructure

High mortality rates due to disease or war

LOW POPULATION GROWTH

Low birth rates

Specific programs aimed at reducing birth rates

Good educational opportunities and access to information, especially for women

The Impact of Overpopulation

Whatever the rate or extent of population growth, it is clear that humans have a huge impact on the planet. As the world population rises, this impact is likely to increase. Whether the Earth can deal with it is still a matter of debate.

Limited World Resources

People disagree over whether humans have reached, or even gone beyond, the limits of Earth's resources, such as food, land, and clean water. Many believe that human impact on the environment is already so damaging that some of it is now irreversible. Others believe that with better management, there are sufficient resources available to sustain further population growth. Whatever the case, the future of the world's resources will depend on new and more advanced technologies than those that are already in place.

Blaming the People

It is easy to assume that most, if not all, problems to do with depletion of resources and damage to the environment are directly related to population pressure. Population numbers alone, however, are not the only factors to consider. For example, North America, with only 5 percent of the world's population, consumes 25 percent of the world's resources. Levels of consumption are therefore also important factors.

CASE STUDY
Easter Island

Rapa Nui (Easter Island) is a small, isolated, 66-square-mile (170-square-kilometer) landmass, located 1,056 miles (3,700 kilometers) west of Chile. Between 1000 and 1650 CE, it is estimated that the island's small population increased rapidly to 15,000 or even 20,000 (about 100 people per 0.4 square mile or square kilometer). By the time the Dutch explorer, Jacob Roggeveen, arrived in 1722, the once palm-covered and productive island was bare. By the end of the nineteenth century, the population was reduced to 132. Many people believe this decline was due to overexploitation of the island's resources, leading to massive deforestation, loss of biodiversity, soil damage, and loss of wood for fuel and construction of fishing boats.

Not everyone agrees with this analysis. Some people suggest that the arrival of European diseases, raiding for slaves, and fighting among the islanders all contributed to the region's decline. Whatever the case, Rapa Nui demonstrates the fragility of the relationship between people and their environment.

◀ Rapa Nui is famous for these statues carved by the islanders up to 1,000 years ago. The decline of the island's population is still a mystery.

▼ A woman in Ningxia, China, waters her crop by hand through holes in moisture-retaining plastic covers. Ningxia is one of the driest regions on Earth.

Vanishing Water

Every human being needs water—not just water, but clean, fresh water—to drink, cook with, and bathe in. Fresh water comes mainly from under the ground and from lakes, rivers, and rainfall. Once it is used, replacing that water is not an easy process.

The state of global freshwater supplies is poor. So much water has been pumped from the ground for agricultural, industrial, and domestic use, that water tables worldwide are falling. Northern China, the Unites States, India, Pakistan, Iran, and Mexico are all seriously affected in this way. Global warming is likely to add to water shortages in some areas as patterns of rainfall change.

No Water, No Food

Removing groundwater and lowering water tables may cause salts from the soil to rise to the surface. On agricultural land, this can result in crop damage. A likely outcome will be eventual food shortages and increases in the price of grain. This is already happening in countries such as China.

Dirty Water

Globally, water is in short supply. Even where it is available, the quality of that water may threaten the lives of those who use it. It is estimated that over one billion people in LEDCs worldwide do not have access to safe drinking water. The main reason for this is poor sanitation. The result may be debilitating waterborne diseases, such as cholera, typhoid, and dysentery. Often, this is due to lack of infrastructure such as water supplies or protected wells. As a country's economy becomes stronger, a larger percentage of its people tend to have access to drinking water and proper sanitation. However, this is not the end of the problem, since the treatment and purification of water is expensive and uses large amounts of energy.

Increasing Demands

It is probable that most of the 3 billion people to be added to the world's population by 2050 will be in areas already experiencing water shortages. These include many LEDCs, particularly in parts of Africa. But water shortages are not just a problem for LEDCs. It is estimated that by 2020, the state of California will be lacking as much water as it consumes today. Los Angeles, the largest city in this coastal desert area, is able to support about 1 million people on its own water. By 2020, it is predicted that there will be 22 million people living in the region.

CASE STUDY
Making More Water

It is possible to extract fresh water from salt water by a process called desalination. The Mediterranean island of Malta already obtains most of its fresh water in this way, as does southern Israel. Israel is a desert country with frequent droughts and a high population density. Desalinated water allows farmers to irrigate the land and produce sufficient crops to support the population. However, desalination is an expensive and energy-intensive process. Unless the energy it uses can be obtained from a renewable (or nuclear) source, it is likely to increase the effects of global warming.

Feed the World

Like water, food is a resource that every human depends on for survival. Yet hunger and malnutrition continue to kill or shorten life on a massive scale. Famine is still a threat, particularly in parts of sub-Saharan Africa. Is there enough food on Earth, or could populations be outgrowing the global food supply? And how will increasing demands for food affect the planet?

Gains and Losses

Thomas Malthus (see page 6) proved how hard it is to predict the food supplies of the future. But what about the food supplies of today? It is clear from the evidence below how improved farming methods have increased food production over the years. However, these changes have not benefited all. The movement from small-scale farming to the mass-production of crops for export, for example, has put local farmers out of business. It has also harmed the environment as soils have been drained of nutrients and chemical fertilizers and pesticides have poisoned habitats.

Evidence

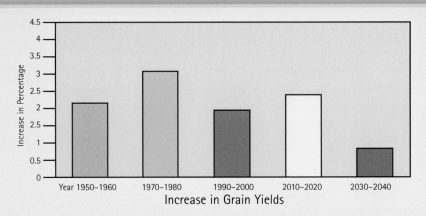

GROWING GRAIN SUPPLIES

The graph shows that grain yields have increased each decade since 1950, particularly during the "green revolution" of the 1950s and 1960s. More recently, the improvement in yields has decreased. In the future, new technologies such as gene modification (GM) may allow a further increase.

Food For All?

Evidence suggests that famine is not linked to population numbers as such, but to other factors. These include natural hazards, particularly drought, which is partly a result of global warming. Another key factor is poor development. Most LEDCs lack the infrastructure they need to get maximum benefit from the land they have available. For example, a more developed infrastructure might include modern equipment, better roads for transporting goods, improved storage facilities, better irrigation, increased trade benefits, and access to effective fertilizers.

Many people argue that the world is not short of food—the problem is that it needs to be distributed more evenly, with global effort to help improve resources for the hungry.

IT'S A FACT

Between 1960 and 2000, the world population doubled from 3 billion to 6 billion. In the same period, the daily calorific intake in LEDCs increased by an estimated 25–30 percent.

▼ Even when food aid is available, it does not always reach its intended destination. Flooded or impassable roads, accidents, or attacks by armed groups often mean that those who are most in need go hungry.

The Fight for Land

The demand for food has a significant effect on the land. Agriculture is said to have replaced a third of temperate and tropical forests, and a quarter of natural grasslands worldwide. It seems inevitable that, as the global population increases, more and more land will be used to grow food. In addition, land is needed to build new homes, transportation networks, and industries. Energy systems, including hydroelectric dams and biofuel crops, such as corn and sugar cane, also take up large amounts of land. Pressure in all of these areas is likely to increase with the rising population. The question is, how much land is it reasonable, and safe, to convert for human use before the global environment suffers? Many people would argue that, in much of the world, this point has already been passed.

▼ When land is cleared for agriculture, the soil is often damaged and is easily washed away.

Losing Land

The conversion of land for human use can have serious consequences. Much productive land is being lost and degraded by poor agricultural practices and forest clearance. Overcultivation, increasingly short "fallow" periods, where land can replenish itself naturally, and the removal of trees that anchor soils, lead to loss of fertility, soil erosion, and desertification. Flooding due to global warming may cause further loss of productive agricultural land.

Doing More with Less

Improvements in land management and crop productivity are possible. It is likely that the next big revolution in food production will be the development of genetically modified (GM) crops. These may be able to grow on degraded, salt-loaded, or arid land—but the real impact of this new technology is difficult to assess.

CASE STUDY
Land Loss in Nigeria

Nigeria, already the most highly populated country in Africa, is undergoing explosive population growth. Its present population of 140 million is expected to more than double by 2050. Average life expectancy in Nigeria is only 47 years, and little more than half the population has access to safe drinking water and sanitation. Nigeria is currently losing 1,350 square miles (3,500 square kilometers) of grazing land and cropland to desert every year because of poor farming practices. Loss of land affects 35 million people in northern Nigeria. Meanwhile, Nigeria's livestock population has grown from 6 million to 66 million since 1950, adding to the pressure on the land.

Energy Use Around the World

The amount of energy used by a region does not always correspond to its population. The United States is home to only 5 percent of the world's population, but it uses 26 percent of global energy. This is closely followed by Europe (22 percent) and then China (15.5 percent). It is likely that China will catch up and probably overtake the two Western regions. This is due both to its massive and expanding population, and to its rapid development into a major industrial power. Other parts of Asia and South America are likely to follow China for the same reasons.

The average Canadian currently uses at least 150 times more commercial energy than the average person in Somalia. High standards of living in MEDCs mean that people demand more energy-guzzling machines and appliances, and rely much more heavily on industrial power. As LEDCs develop, their citizens are likely to need greater access to energy and other resources, too. The implications for the planet, however, could be severe.

Evidence

WORLD ENERGY CONSUMPTION

This bar chart shows the top energy users around the world. The United States is the top consumer of energy. Despite its enormous population, India uses relatively little energy compared to China or the United States, but this is likely to change rapidly as India becomes more industrialized.

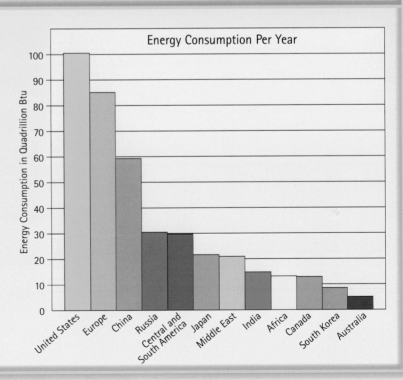

Fossil Fuels

Fossil fuels are currently the world's major energy source, providing 85 percent of total energy consumption. However, these fuels are nonrenewable. If people continue to use them at the current rate—or a higher rate, as populations grow and develop—they will soon run out. In addition, the widespread burning of fossil fuels is almost certainly causing a warming of the Earth's atmosphere and oceans, leading to changes in climate. This in turn is beginning to melt the polar ice caps, affecting sea levels, weather patterns, agriculture, and natural habitats.

Energy Alternatives

Concerns related to fossil fuel use are driving changes toward renewable forms of energy such as water, wind, and solar power. Other renewable energy options include biofuels and sustainably produced hydrogen. There is also a revived interest in nuclear power. Many countries with existing nuclear power programs are debating whether, and to what extent, they should continue to develop these programs. There are concerns about the true cost of nuclear energy and about the safety of the technology. However, many new nuclear sites are being developed in LEDCs. Currently, 168 sites are either being built or planned, most in rapidly developing regions such as Vietnam, Indonesia, and Turkey.

CASE STUDY
Living Fuel

In the future, fuel may be manufactured by artificial life forms created out of synthetic DNA. The DNA will be added to bacteria, programming them to produce biofuels such as methane or hydrogen gas. These can be used as alternatives to fossil fuels. The bacteria can be grown on food mediums ranging from cellulose (plant) fiber to household waste and even old car tires! They may, therefore, represent a more sustainable energy source for the future.

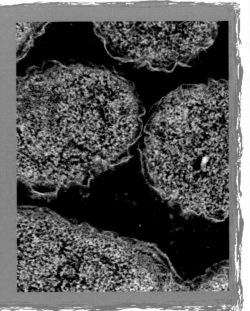

Population and the Environment

Humans have always had an impact on the environment—for example, clearing land for agriculture has shaped landscapes for thousands of years. However, only since the twentieth century have the impacts of human activity really reached a global scale. Examples include the mass destruction of rain forests, pollution of the world's oceans, and damage to the atmosphere, particularly in the form of global warming.

Human activity has also increased rates of extinction among certain plant and animal species. Although estimates vary widely, it is thought that 4–8 percent of rain-forest species could be extinct by 2015, and 17–35 percent by 2040. Some predictions suggest that a majority of all species, particularly larger land animals, could be wiped from the world by the end of the twenty-first century.

IT'S A FACT

Half of all coastal ecosystems are now under pressure due to high population densities and urban development.

CASE STUDY
Deforestation in Madagascar

Between 1990 and 2005, Central America lost nearly 20 percent of its rain forest, South America almost 7 percent, Southeast Asia 12.5 percent, and Africa 10 percent. One of the worst-affected countries is Madagascar, a large island off the southeast coast of Africa. Massive deforestation there has resulted in soil loss and desertification, and has disrupted the natural water cycle, leading to the degradation of water sources. Almost 90 percent of productive land has been affected in this way. In 2006, Madagascar introduced a scheme to create protected areas that allow some use, while preserving natural habitats. For example, Strict Nature Reserves do not allow any access, but National Parks can support local communities while encouraging a developing tourist trade.

Population and Technology

Over the last 100 years, new technologies, such as the fuel-burning engine, power stations, the chainsaw, and modern agricultural methods and machinery, have vastly increased the rate at which environmental change has come about. Even so, some of the greatest impacts on the environment have been in poorer areas where large numbers of people have caused environmental damage without the intervention of modern techniques. For example, clearing of tropical forest by slash-and-burn techniques in order for people to grow crops, is the single biggest cause of tropical forest destruction. This does not mean that people, or population numbers, are necessarily to blame. The culprits are often poor rural communities who have been displaced from their land by logging companies or large plantation owners.

▼ Open-pit mining can damage large areas of land that might otherwise be used for purposes such as food production.

For Better or Worse?

Of course, new technologies can bring many benefits as well as disadvantages. This is especially true of the development of alternative energy sources (see page 27) and increased food supplies (page 22). For example, the Food and Agriculture Organisation (FAO) has estimated that meeting future food needs will depend 70 percent on better technologies and increased yields, 20 percent on better storage and distribution, and only 10 percent on increased land use. At the same time, medical advances have improved life expectancy and the quality of life for billions of people.

Yet, it remains the case that the use of modern technology has transformed the world, often with destructive outcomes. Development may tend to lower birth and death rates, but increased wealth and technological capacity brings its own problems. The exploration and extraction of energy, the proliferation of waste (and places to dispose of it), and modern agricultural developments are all evidence of exploiting the land. This raises an important question; as the world population increases, can modern technology assist people in their need to find better ways of coping. Or does technology become another way in which they add to the planet's already growing problems?

Populations on the Move

Migrations, or movements of people from place to place to live, have taken place throughout history. Most have been made by people seeking a better quality of life. Migrations are not necessarily the result of overpopulation—they may be triggered, for example, by war or other sufferings. However, they often stem from a lack of resources, such as land, work opportunities, or food. Often migrations involve the movement of the rural poor into cities (see page 32). Some migrations are made illegally, by people so desperate that they will risk everything for the chance of a better life.

Two-way Impact

Where migration takes place between two nations, both countries may benefit. For example, there are more than 25 million people

CASE STUDY
Desperate Journeys

Every year, hundreds of thousands of people set off on grueling journeys to escape a life of poverty and seek a new start elsewhere. Some succeed. Others end up a little better off than they were, BUT some do not make it at all. In August 2007, a small, open fishing boat was intercepted by a Greek tug in the northern Mediterranean Sea. Crammed on board were 28 migrants from Africa. As the tug approached to rescue them, the migrants moved to one side and their boat capsized. Only three survived. Hundreds of African migrants, bound for the shores of Europe, die in this way each year. They form just a fraction of the vast number of people around the world who lack access to the basic resources they need.

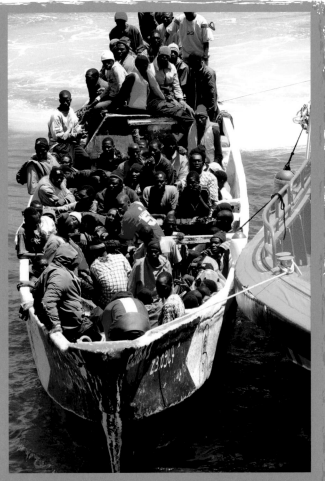

▲ A boat heavily laden with refugees is intercepted by the authorities. The refugees will be sent back to their country of origin, but desperation will mean they will try to find a better life again.

of Mexican origin living (both legally and illegally) in the United States. Each year Mexican immigrants send $9 billion back to family members in Mexico, while spending $82 billion on goods, services, and taxes in the U.S.A.

On the negative side, migrations may alter the balance of populations, create tensions between local people and migrants, and put pressure on resources that previously met local needs. Migration may also result in the loss of qualified people, such as doctors and nurses, or skilled laborers from countries who arguably need their skills more than the receiver countries. These are difficult issues that have to be addressed in a world of growing populations and increased mobility.

The Rise of the City

In 1800, only 3 percent of the world's population lived in cities. By the end of the twentieth century, almost 50 percent did so. By 2030, it is estimated that 60 percent— or three out five people—will live in urban areas. Many will have arrived from surrounding rural areas, unable to maintain a living from the land and in search of work, shelter, or protection.

The increase will be greatest in the poorest, and currently, least-urbanized continents—Asia and Africa. These are also two regions where the greatest overall population increases are expected. Even now, 1 billion people live in desperately poor outer-city areas called shanty towns. These are often built of corrugated iron and plastic sheeting, and have no proper sanitation or basic healthcare facilities. Social problems, such as crime, drug addiction, alcoholism, poverty, and unemployment, are rife and life expectancy is short. By 2030, over 2 billion people will be living in similar slums.

IT'S A FACT

In 1950, there were 83 cities with populations greater than a million; by 2007, this had risen to 468.

▼ Overcrowding, poor sanitation, lack of education, and crime make urban living such as this a difficult way of life.

City Limits

The future of the urban poor is strongly tied to the future of the world's population as a whole. In 2007, the UN put forward three "policy initiatives" that would make a huge difference to the social, economic, and environmental living conditions of a majority of the world's population.

The first of these was respect for the rights of the poor to the city. This includes advances in social development, such as promoting the rights of women, making education universally available, and meeting health needs, including those related to reproduction. The second initiative was concern for the land needs of the poor. This means ensuring poor families in cities have access to space, water, sewerage systems, power, and transportation (rather than denying them these facilities, as often happens currently). The final initiative was support for community organizations and social movements in improving the nature of future urban expansion. This involves working with others to reduce poverty and promote environmental awareness.

It remains to be seen whether the UN's recommendations can be put into practice; if not, the world's growing cities will add to, rather than combat, poverty and human misery.

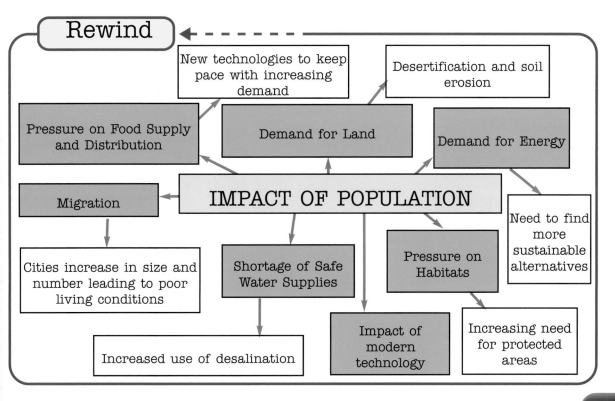

Managing Populations

It seems likely that the consequences of global population growth will be severe for the Earth. But how should the populations of the future be managed? It is important to look at population problems at a regional level before human impact can be lessened for the planet as a whole.

A Matter of Numbers?

The UN estimates that 850 million people in the world today are malnourished or starving, and more than a billion lack access to safe drinking water. Some people may argue, therefore, that the Earth is unable to support its present numbers, let alone cope with future rises in population. Others suggest that poverty was worse in the past when populations were much smaller.

Evidence

MALNUTRITION AROUND THE WORLD

This map shows that the northern regions of the world are largely free from malnutrition, but large areas of Southeast Asia and Central and South America still have moderate levels. Parts of Africa, however, particularly south of the Sahara, show very high, and unacceptable, levels of malnutrition.

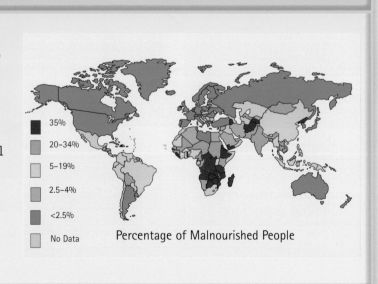

35%
20–34%
5–19%
2.5–4%
<2.5%
No Data

Percentage of Malnourished People

Government Trouble

As we have seen, there can be poverty without overpopulation. For example, Zimbabwe has a low population density and plenty of productive land, yet it suffers from extreme poverty and environmental degradation. This has been largely brought about by corrupt and oppressive government policies. In particular, the grabbing of farmland by the government in the 1990s and early 2000s meant that farms were no longer properly managed and fell into disrepair. This severely jeopardized food supplies.

North and South Korea offer another example. Both have similar population densities and natural resources, but although South Korea enjoys the benefits of a modern, developed state, North Korea remains a poor and undeveloped country, largely due to its repressive government.

Additional Factors

Bad governments—those that are corrupt, ineffective, incompetent, or a combination of the three—and bad economic policies can certainly cause poverty and hunger. But this does not mean that all poor, or overpopulated, countries have bad governments. There are many factors, including war, drought, and other natural disasters, that create conditions in which poverty may flourish. Whatever the cause, the more people that are born into these conditions, the larger the population of world poor becomes.

▲ The seizing of farms by the Zimbabwean government meant that local people could no longer farm their land. As a result, much of Zimbabwe's productive farmland now lies uncultivated and food is in short supply.

Who Needs Children?

While poverty continues to overwhelm many LEDCs, the majority of people in MEDCs experience a much higher standard of living. It is argued that in these countries, family sizes start to drop as the cost of living and life expectancy increases. We have already seen that many Western regions are experiencing zero or negative population growth.

As well as the changing roles of women, the expense of bringing up children, and modern marriage patterns, there is a more fundamental reason for lowering birth rates. In an industrialized society, the "need" for children is less. In many poor and rural economies, children provide an important part of the labor force where most of the work is agricultural. In industrial societies, this is no longer the case. Also, in many poorer societies, having more children is seen as an insurance against old age. The children become carers for their elders, as well as replacement workers.

In some countries, low birth rates cause a problem—sometimes called the demographic time bomb. With fewer children, and longer life expectancies, populations overall start to age. This puts greater stresses on social services and healthcare systems. Economic problems start to occur as the number of people of working age declines. One solution to the demographic time bomb is planned immigration. Many MEDCs actively encourage such immigration as a way of ensuring a young and active workforce to support their ageing population.

▼ Senior citizens enjoy a game of bingo in Phoenix, Arizona. Rich countries tend to have aging populations and declining numbers in the workforce. This can lead to skills shortages and to rising care costs.

Ever Growing

In most countries in Africa, Asia, and Latin America, the opposite situation is true. There, birth rates are still well above what is known as the replacement rate—that is the number of births it takes in one generation to ensure an equal number of people in the next generation. In many LEDCs, the proportion of people under the age of 15 is as high as 45–50 percent. These are the parentsof tomorrow. Birth rates in LEDCs are declining overall, but each new generation will still be greater than the previous one, simply because it is based on larger numbers of people. Even if birth rates fall to replacement levels, it will take another 70 years before population growth stops.

Evidence

POPULATION PYRAMIDS

Population figures are often shown as pyramids. These two population pyramids are for France (an MEDC) and India (an LEDC). In India, the pyramid has a much broader base and narrow tip, indicating a high birth rate, but also high mortality and low life expectancy. In France, the opposite is true. Birth rates are low, but survival rates are very high, leading to a more "top heavy" structure and a much higher percentage of older people.

A Gap to Close

The ultimate aim of any population policy must be to reach a point where everyone on Earth has at least a reasonable quality of life, with access to sufficient resources to meet his or her needs. For everyone to enjoy a similar standard of living in the world today, we would require another two-and-a-half planets. So how can a balance in population and resources be reached?

▼ Better health monitoring and care mean that people in richer countries are staying active for longer; this means they can work productively to a greater age.

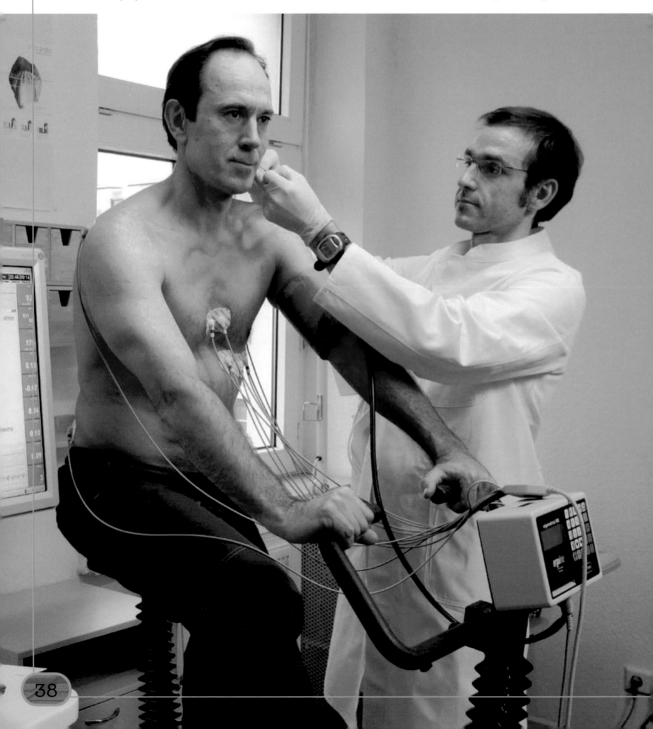

Demographic Transition

Half a century ago, demographers began to develop and discuss ideas about how a balance in population might occur. Based on changes in the industrializing nations of the nineteenth century, they predicted an eventual shift from high birth rates and death rates to lower birth and death rates worldwide. Better basic sanitation and healthcare, reduced infant mortality, and improvements in education (particularly among women), would combine with better life prospects to lower birth rates and increase life expectancy. This is the "demographic transition" that is now occurring in many MEDCs (see page 37).

Balancing Out?

In MEDCs, the "break-even" point for a population comes at a replacement rate of about 2.1 children per couple. Such levels were achieved several decades ago in much of Europe. In Italy, the replacement rate is now as low as 1.28, and in Poland, it is 1.25. Australia and Canada are higher at 1.76 and 1.61 respectively. All these figures point to a steady population decline. However, increasing length of life means that these declines will be less than 10 percent by 2050.

The United States is an exception among MEDCs. With a replacement rate of 2.09 and a high rate of immigration, the population is still growing by 1 percent per year. Similar observations apply to the United Kingdom and Australia—despite replacement rates around 1.71, high levels of immigration suggest there will be significant population increases in both countries over the next few decades.

As we have already seen on pages 30–31, migration can present both benefits and difficulties to countries "donating" and receiving migrating populations. One recent phenomenon that has been observed is that, as donor countries become better off themselves, people who have left the country concerned begin to migrate back to their country of origin. It is therefore not always easy to predict the outcomes of these global movements.

CASE STUDY
One-Child China

In 1979, the new Chinese leader, Deng Xiaoping, saw China's massive and rapidly growing population as a barrier to economic development. He began a national program of "birth planning," encouraging families to have only one child. This limit has been strongly enforced in urban areas. In rural areas, families are allowed two children if the first child is a girl. Additional children result in large fines and other penalties. With its one-child policy, the fertility rate of women in China has fallen from 5 to 1.7 births.

China considers its policy a success. The government points out that the restrictions have saved many millions of children from lives of poverty and misery. Despite its huge population, China has been more successful than most developing countries in limiting its population growth. Many observers, however, consider the policy to be an abuse of human and reproductive rights. They also point to the kind of social and demographic problems that China is now experiencing, such as aging populations.

▼ A mural promotes China's one-child policy. This family looks happy, but many people oppose a system that forces families to limit their size to three people.

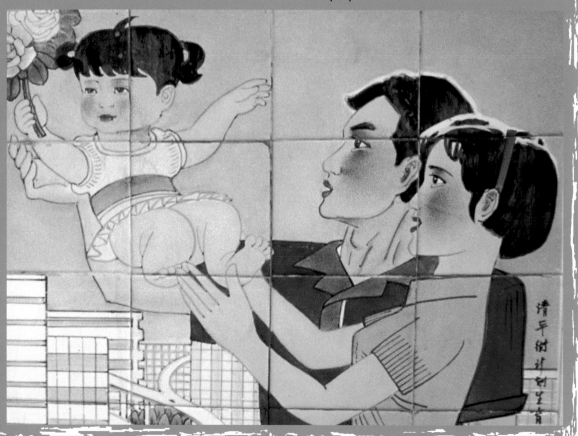

An Ideal Limit?

A recent study, carried out at Stanford University in California, suggested that an ideal global population was around 2 billion. This was based on many factors, including sensible resource use, development of current technologies, and a closing of the gap between the rich and the poor. This figure is less than one-third of today's population and is about the same as it was in the 1930s.

Other experts suggest that populations could comfortably reach tens of billions of people. They argue that any poor country could achieve Western standards of living if it chose, for example, to let people own their own land, develop modern agriculture and industry, and make use of alternative energy and desalinization.

Although these are dramatically different estimates, they both suggest that the key to sustaining the world's population is through appropriate development—that is, to increase quality of life through the better use and management of the world's resources. Increasing people's wealth and prosperity tends to have two other vital effects—one is a lowering of the birth rate, leading to an eventual decline in population numbers. The other is a greater ability—and commitment—to address environmental problems.

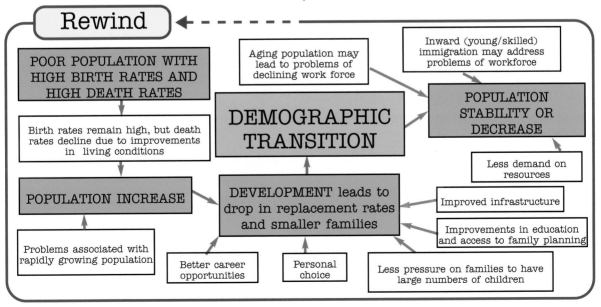

Rewind

POOR POPULATION WITH HIGH BIRTH RATES AND HIGH DEATH RATES

Birth rates remain high, but death rates decline due to improvements in living conditions

POPULATION INCREASE

Problems associated with rapidly growing population

Aging population may lead to problems of declining work force

DEMOGRAPHIC TRANSITION

DEVELOPMENT leads to drop in replacement rates and smaller families

Better career opportunities

Personal choice

Less pressure on families to have large numbers of children

Inward (young/skilled) immigration may address problems of workforce

POPULATION STABILITY OR DECREASE

Less demand on resources

Improved infrastructure

Improvements in education and access to family planning

What the Future Holds

The Earth is at a critical point in its long history. It is clear that the current situation is an unsustainable one. Changes need to occur, and to occur rapidly, if the Earth is to survive. These include the appropriate development of LEDCs, more assistance to LEDCs by MEDCs, better governance (how the world runs its affairs), and more careful consumption of the Earth's resources.

Development of LEDCs

Population increases tend to be greatest in LEDCs. Although these countries should be encouraged to develop more rapidly, this should be done in a sustainable way. This includes improvements in infrastructure, such as transportation systems, health services, energy solutions, and particularly education. In addition, greater access to land (property rights) would encourage more responsible and productive use of land by local communities.

Assistance from MEDCs

It is in the interests of richer countries to assist in the development of poorer parts of the world. As LEDCs become more

self-sufficient and more prosperous, all available evidence suggests that population growth will decline.

Help can be channeled through existing organizations, such as the UN. Any scheme must be focused on clear objectives and closely monitored to make sure it is having the desired effects. For example, there should be accurate monitoring of improvements in educational opportunities and standards, and steps to ensure that funding finds its way to appropriate local organizations.

Better Governance

There is a need for better "governance" worldwide.
It has been demonstrated that bad government—often worsened by war, corruption, and internal conflict—can cause poverty and environmental degradation just as much as overpopulation. The recent example of Zimbabwe shows what can happen when corrupt governments remain unchallenged. Many people now accept that the international community, including other African nations, should have done much more, at an earlier stage, to put pressure on the government to change. Policies need to be addressed at all levels, however, from local to international. The latter would include fairer trade agreements that allow poorer countries greater access to international markets. This would ensure that they received the greatest benefit from their own resources.

Careful Consumption

The world as a whole, and particularly the West, needs to tackle the issue of consumption. MEDCs are often criticized for their excessive use of resources, particularly at the expense of poorer countries and their environments. Although it may not be realistic to expect people in rich countries to lower their living standards, it is realistic to continue to develop ways of reducing their environmental impact. There are many ways of doing this. They include renewable energy use and energy conservation, improving natural habitats, much greater recycling of resources, and reduction in use of materials and processes that harm the environment.

◀ This solar stove works by focusing the Sun's rays on the cooking pot. This means that less wood is used unsustainably as fuel. Technologies such as these can help poorer countries to develop more sustainably.

Global Give and Take

We have seen that shrinking populations can cause difficulties of their own—for example, the problems of a declining workforce. This could be managed by planned migration, as long as it did not disadvantage the countries from which migrants were coming. In addition, a process called globalization is taking place, whereby goods and services produced in one part of the word are made increasingly available in others. This means that more and more skilled jobs will be "outsourced" from MEDCs to LEDCs, where there are large numbers of young people, many well educated.

Both globalization and migration should contribute to the development of poor countries and help to narrow the global rich-poor income gap. As a further effect, this will bring increased opportunities for education and jobs, especially for women in LEDCs. Birth rates, in turn, are likely to fall.

▼ Call centers based in poorer countries can use the skills of educated young people more cheaply than in rich countries, where skill shortages may exist. However, not everyone supports the globalization of employment opportunities.

Future Perfect?

A world with fewer people would put less pressure on Earth's resources than one with a high and rapidly expanding population. But the issue of population remains a highly complex one. It is easy to jump to conclusions or make assumptions that may not be justified. Better governance worldwide, a fairer distribution of the world's resources, and above all, a more sustainable approach to how people live, will allow this and future generations to find a better balance with the Earth.

Everyone has a role to play in this. The future population of the world is not just determined by the choices that individuals make about the size of family they have. It is about the way the world develops. What people do, what they buy, how they behave toward the environment—are all part of that process.

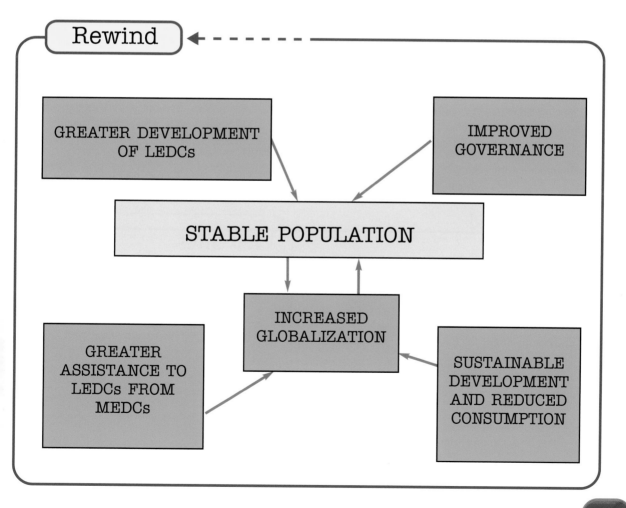

Glossary, Further Information, and Web Sites

Biofuel Fuel made from plants grown on plantations, agricultural by-products, or from domestic or agricultural waste.

Consumption The using up of resources, such as fuel and water. Levels of consumption are not equal, and are generally higher in MEDCs than in LEDCs.

DNA Deoxyribonucleic acid. The the genetic material that determines the makeup of all living cells.

Famine An extreme scarcity of food due to climatic or other factors.

Fossil fuels The coal, oil, and gas that has formed over millions of years from the remains of plants and animals.

Genetic modification Changing the characteristics of an organism, such as a plant or animal, by altering its DNA or genetic makeup.

Globalization The process of extending communications, trade and the movement of people to a global dimension. For example, goods produced in one country are made available in another.

Infrastructure The buildings, transportation systems, communications, and services that support an area.

Livestock Farm animals, including cattle, sheep, and pigs.

Malnourished Lacking the essential food needed to be healthy.

Renewable sources Energy and other resources that do not run out with use.

Sanitation The safe disposal of sewage and refuse from people's homes.

Slash-and-burn A type of land clearance where people cut down woods and forests and then burn the remains to create farmland.

Sustainable Carried out without depleting or permanently damaging resources.

Temperate forest Nontropical forest found in Western Europe, Northeast Asia, and parts of North America. Deciduous trees are common in temperate forest.

Tropical forest The forest found in the tropical parts of the world, such as Africa, South America, and Southeast Asia, on or near the equator.

Books to read

Africa, Progress and Problems:
Population and Overcrowding
Tunde Obadina (Mason Crest Publishers, 2006)

An Overcrowded World
Rob Bowden (Raintree, 2002)

Earth's Changing Landscape: Population Growth
Philip Steele (Smart Apple Media, 2004)

Populations and Ecosystems
Susan Glass (Perfection Learning, 2005)

Web Sites

Due to the changing nature of Internet links, Rosen Publishing has developed an online list of Web sites related to the subject of this book. This site is regularly updated. Please use this link to access this list: www.rosenlinks.com/ces/popu

Topic Web

Use this topic web to discover themes and ideas in subjects that are related to population.

English and Literacy

- Write eyewitness accounts of how people cope during droughts and famines.
- Debate the pros and cons of whether famines are a result of overpopulation.
- Debate the pros and cons of planned migration.

Science and Environment

- Discuss diet and nutrition in relation to poor communities in both MEDCs and LEDCs.
- Look at the impact of overpopulation on ecosystems.
- Understand the science behind renewable energy sources, such as nuclear power, solar power, and fuel cell technology.

History and Economics

- Study how societies change over time giving evidence for demographic transition.
- Look at migrations and ways in which they have influenced host and donor countries.

Overpopulation

Art and Culture

- Discuss the effect of religion and culture on different societies, particularly in relation to family size.
- Look at how poor communities and cultures view their own circumstances through art and music.

Geography

- Look at the distribution and density of populations in relation to natural resources.
- Discuss trade in relation to MEDCs and LEDCs.
- Look at sustainable development and its role in helping LEDCs improve their economies and infrastructure.

Index